EXPLORING THE STATES

Idaho

THE GEM STATE

by Patrick Perish

BELLWETHER MEDIA · MINNEAPOLIS, MN

Note to Librarians, Teachers, and Parents:

Blastoff! Readers are carefully developed by literacy experts and combine standards-based content with developmentally appropriate text.

Level 1 provides the most support through repetition of high-frequency words, light text, predictable sentence patterns, and strong visual support.

Level 2 offers early readers a bit more challenge through varied simple sentences, increased text load, and less repetition of high-frequency words.

Level 3 advances early-fluent readers toward fluency through increased text and concept load, less reliance on visuals, longer sentences, and more literary language.

Level 4 builds reading stamina by providing more text per page, increased use of punctuation, greater variation in sentence patterns, and increasingly challenging vocabulary.

Level 5 encourages children to move from "learning to read" to "reading to learn" by providing even more text, varied writing styles, and less familiar topics.

Whichever book is right for your reader, Blastoff! Readers are the perfect books to build confidence and encourage a love of reading that will last a lifetime!

This edition first published in 2014 by Bellwether Media, Inc.

No part of this publication may be reproduced in whole or in part without written permission of the publisher. For information regarding permission, write to Bellwether Media, Inc., Attention: Permissions Department, 5357 Penn Avenue South, Minneapolis, MN 55419.

Library of Congress Cataloging-in-Publication Data

Perish, Patrick.
Idaho / by Patrick Perish.
    pages cm. – (Blastoff! readers. Exploring the states)
Includes bibliographical references and index.
Summary: "Developed by literacy experts for students in grades three through seven, this book introduces young readers to the geography and culture of Idaho"– Provided by publisher.
ISBN 978-1-62617-011-7 (hardcover : alk. paper)
1. Idaho–Juvenile literature. I. Title.
F746.3.P47 2014
979.6–dc23

2013003497

Printed in the United States of America, North Mankato, MN.

Table of Contents

Where Is Idaho?

Idaho is located in the northwestern United States. It is the fourteenth largest state. The capital of Idaho is Boise. It sits in the southwestern part of the state.

Idaho touches the Canadian **province** of British Columbia to the north. To the northeast is Montana. The **Continental Divide** forms part of this boundary. Idaho borders Wyoming in the southeast. Utah and Nevada are the state's neighbors to the south. On its western side lie Oregon and Washington. The Snake River forms part of the western boundary.

Washington

Oregon

Pacific Ocean

British Columbia

Continental Divide

N
W   E
S

Montana

Idaho

Meridian

Craters of the
Moon National
Monument

Nampa ★ Boise

Idaho
Falls

Wyoming

Snake River

Nevada

Utah

Native American tribes called Idaho home long before Europeans arrived. In 1805, Meriwether Lewis and William Clark passed through Idaho while exploring the West. The discovery of gold in 1860 brought many people to the area. Idaho's population was almost 90,000 when it became a state in 1890.

panning for gold

Idaho Timeline!

1805: Lewis and Clark explore Idaho on their great journey through the West.

1846: The United States gains land that includes Idaho in the Oregon Treaty.

1855: The Nez Perce Indian Reservation is created.

1860: Gold is discovered in northern Idaho.

1863: The Idaho Territory is created.

1874: The Utah Northern Railroad is the first railroad to enter Idaho.

1890: Idaho becomes the forty-third state.

1924: Craters of the Moon National Monument and Preserve is established.

1976: Teton Dam on the Teton River collapses. Flooding results in eleven deaths and millions of dollars of damage.

Nez Perce Indian Reservation

Lewis and Clark

Utah Northern Railroad

The Land

The rugged Rocky Mountains cover most of Idaho. They run down from Canada through the **panhandle** and along the state's eastern border. Borah Peak in central Idaho is the highest point at 12,662 feet (3,859 meters). Weather in the mountains is cool and wet year-round. The state's lowlands have warm summers and cold winters.

The Snake River sweeps west across southern Idaho. Running along it on both sides is the Snake River **Plain**. Most farming in the state takes place here. In western Idaho, the Snake River curves north toward Washington. It forms part of the border with Oregon as it flows through Hells **Canyon**.

Hells Canyon

Idaho's Climate
average °F

spring
Low: 38°
High: 61°

summer
Low: 55°
High: 85°

fall
Low: 39°
High: 62°

winter
Low: 24°
High: 39°

Did you know?
At 7,900 feet (2,400 meters) deep, Hells Canyon is the deepest canyon in North America.

Craters of the Moon

Did you know?

Eruptions occur at Craters of the Moon every 2,000 years or so. The last was over 2,000 years ago. The next lava flow could come at any time.

In south-central Idaho lies a dry and **barren** landscape. It is known as Craters of the Moon National Monument and Preserve. Around 15,000 years ago, **volcanoes** began spilling lava over the land. This melted rock slowly cooled and hardened to create the landscape.

Craters of the Moon is surprisingly full of life. Tough shrubs and wildflowers dig their roots into cracks in the rock. Birds and small animals also find ways to survive here. Many visitors come each year to see the harsh beauty of the lava fields.

yellow-pine chipmunk

wildflowers

Wildlife

The wilderness of Idaho is home to a variety of life. In the panhandle, western white pines and other **conifers** blanket the mountains. Grizzly bears and wolverines roam the woods in search of food. Trout and salmon swim in the cold waters of Idaho's fast-flowing rivers.

Mountain lions stalk bighorn sheep in the state's deep canyons. The peregrine falcon makes its nest on high cliffs. It dives at incredible speeds to catch pigeons, doves, and other small birds. Sage grouses in the southern plains attract mates with a unique dance. They strut and puff out their chests to make a popping sound.

grizzly bear

mountain lion

sage grouse

peregrine falcon

Landmarks

Natural wonders are the biggest attractions in the Gem State. Bruneau **Dunes** State Park sits in southwestern Idaho. Its tallest dune rises 470 feet (143 meters). Hagerman **Fossil** Beds National Monument is known for its fossils of early horses. It also has fossils of saber-toothed tigers and giant sloths!

The Museum of Idaho in Idaho Falls has exhibits on the history of the West. One tells the story of Lewis and Clark in Idaho. It features a model of the explorers' boat and a life-size Native American village. In the town of Blackfoot is the Idaho Potato Museum. Visitors can learn all about Idaho's most famous vegetable.

Bruneau Dunes State Park

Shoshone Falls

Did you know?

On the Snake River near Twin Falls, the mighty Shoshone Falls plummets 212 feet (65 meters). It is sometimes called the "Niagara of the West."

Boise

Did you know?
The name *Boise* comes from a French word meaning "wooded."

Boise sits on the banks of the Boise River. It was founded by French-Canadian fur **trappers** in the 1800s. In its early years, the city was an important **crossroads**. People passed through Boise as they followed the **Oregon Trail** west. Others passed through on the way to mining camps.

Boise Art Museum

Idaho State Capitol

Today, Boise is the capital and largest city in Idaho. More than 200,000 people call it home. There are many fun attractions in Boise. At Zoo Boise, visitors can see everything from sloth bears to wallabies up close. The Boise Art Museum features paintings, pottery, and other artwork from around the world.

Working

Did you know?
Idaho grows more potatoes than any other state.

Gold was discovered in northern Idaho in 1860. Since then, mining has been an important activity in the state. Idaho is one of the top silver producers in the country. Zinc, copper, and lead are also mined in the state. Idaho factories turn these **natural resources** into usable goods.

In the state's vast pine forests, loggers cut down trees for lumber. Many farmers along the Snake River raise cattle or sheep. Others grow wheat, hay, and sugar beets. The state's most famous crop is the Idaho potato. Many Idahoans have **service jobs**. They serve the state's visitors at **resorts**, lodges, and restaurants. Other service workers have jobs in banks, shops, and hospitals.

Where People Work in Idaho

government
14%

services
82%

farming and
natural resources
2%

manufacturing
2%

Playing

skiing at
Sun Valley

Idahoans love nothing more than the great outdoors. Each year, thousands of guests hit the slopes at the famous Sun Valley ski resort. The state's mighty rivers invite fishers to cast their lines for steelhead trout and other large fish. Idahoans also enjoy hiking, mountain climbing, and camping throughout state and national parks.

fly fishing

Boise State Broncos football field

City life in Idaho is just as exciting. Many Idahoans attend plays and orchestra concerts. Sports fans love to cheer for the Boise State Broncos. Their famous blue football field is a thrilling place to see a game.

Food

lamb stew

salmon

Did you know?
In the Basque Block of Boise, visitors can try lamb stew, pea soup, and other traditional Basque dishes.

Idaho foods reflect the resources of the land. Dishes often make use of local **game** such as deer and pheasants. Trout and salmon are also featured in many meals. Idaho potatoes can be boiled, mashed, fried, or baked. Picking wild huckleberries has long been a favorite activity in the state. The berries are used in pies and jams.

Over the years, **immigrants** have brought their favorite foods to Idaho. These dishes have become part of Idaho cooking. Welsh immigrants bake a special raisin bread called *bara brith*. Basques from Spain and France introduced a spicy sausage called *chorizo*.

Homemade French Fries

Ingredients:

4 large potatoes, well scrubbed

Olive oil or cooking oil

Salt as needed

Directions:

1. Preheat oven to 350°F.

2. Cut each potato into eight lengthwise wedges.

3. Put wedges in a mixing bowl and toss with oil.

4. Place wedges in an ungreased baking pan.

5. Bake 20 minutes. Remove potatoes from the oven and turn them over with a spatula. Return the potatoes to the oven and bake for another 10 minutes, or until golden.

6. Sprinkle with salt and serve hot.

Festivals

Shoshone-Bannock
Festival

Many exciting festivals and gatherings take place in Idaho. The National Old-Time Fiddlers' Contest and Festival is held every June in Weiser. Fiddlers from all over the country come to compete and share their love of old-time music.

Lake Coeur D'Alene holiday light display

Lake Coeur D'Alene has one of the largest holiday light displays in the country. Each winter, visitors head to the lake town to see dazzling fireworks and a parade. In Boise, Idahoans can enjoy comedies and dramas at the Idaho Shakespeare Festival. Plays are performed throughout the summer in an outdoor theater.

The Potato State

Potatoes were originally grown by the **Incas** in the highlands of South America. After spreading throughout Europe, the potato came to Idaho in 1836. During Idaho's gold rush, farmers sold potatoes to hungry miners. The potato business was born.

Idaho's high **altitude** and sunny climate are perfect for growing potatoes. Most are grown along the Snake River Plain. Idaho is famous for the Russet Burbank potato. This variety stores well and is delicious baked or fried. The potato is an important symbol of Idaho's rich land and hardworking people.

Russet Burbank potatoes

Fast Facts About Idaho

Idaho's Flag

Idaho's state flag has a blue background. The state seal is in the center, trimmed in gold. The seal shows a woman holding scales and a spear. She symbolizes justice and liberty. Other images on the seal include a miner, an elk, a mountain landscape, and farm produce. These represent the state's beauty and natural resources.

State Animal
Appaloosa

State Nicknames:	The Gem State Gem of the Mountains
State Motto:	*Esto Perpetua;* "Let It Endure Forever"
Year of Statehood:	1890
Capital City:	Boise
Other Major Cities:	Nampa, Meridian, Idaho Falls
Population:	1,567,582 (2010)
Area:	83,569 square miles (216,443 square kilometers); Idaho is the 14th largest state.
Major Industries:	mining, farming, lumber, manufacturing, services
Natural Resources:	silver, gold, zinc, copper, lead, phosphate, lumber
State Government:	70 representatives; 35 senators
Federal Government:	2 representatives; 2 senators
Electoral Votes:	4

State Bird
mountain bluebird

State Flower
syringa

Glossary

altitude—distance above sea level

barren—having few to no trees or other plants

canyon—a narrow river valley with steep, tall sides

conifers—trees that have needles and produce cones

Continental Divide—a ridge of mountains in North America that divides the flow of water; waters east of the divide flow toward the Atlantic Ocean, and waters west of the divide flow toward the Pacific Ocean.

crossroads—a place where two or more roads meet, or a central meeting place

dunes—hills of sand

fossil—the remains of an ancient plant or animal that has been preserved in stone

game—wild animals hunted for food or sport

immigrants—people who leave one country to live in another country

Incas—ancient peoples of South America

native—originally from a specific place

natural resources—materials in the earth that are taken out and used to make products or fuel

Oregon Trail—a route extending more than 2,000 miles (3,219 kilometers) from Missouri to Oregon; pioneers traveled west on the trail between 1840 and 1860.

panhandle—a narrow part of a state that extends from the main area

plain—a large area of flat land

province—an area within a country; provinces follow all the laws of the country and make some of their own laws.

resorts—vacation spots that offer recreation, entertainment, and relaxation

service jobs—jobs that perform tasks for people or businesses

trappers—people who trapped animals to sell their fur

volcanoes—holes in the earth; when a volcano erupts, hot, melted rock called lava shoots out.

To Learn More

AT THE LIBRARY

Brown, Cynthia L. *Geology of the Pacific Northwest: Investigate How the Earth Was Formed with 15 Projects*. White River Junction, Vt.: Nomad Press, 2011.

Dwyer, Helen. *Nez Perce History and Culture*. New York, N.Y.: Gareth Stevens Pub., 2012.

Tieck, Sarah. *Idaho*. Minneapolis, Minn.: ABDO Pub. Co., 2013.

ON THE WEB

Learning more about Idaho is as easy as 1, 2, 3.

1. Go to www.factsurfer.com.

2. Enter "Idaho" into the search box.

3. Click the "Surf" button and you will see a list of related Web sites.

With factsurfer.com, finding more information is just a click away.

Index

The images in this book are reproduced through the courtesy of: Stock Connection/ SuperStock, front cover (bottom); Imagebroker.com/ Heinz-Dieter Falkenstein/ Glow Images, p. 6; Heeb Christian/ Glow Images, p. 7 (left); John Kropewnicki, p. 7 (middle); Metrodyne/ Wikipedia, p. 7 (right); Thinair28, pp. 8-9; Jason Patrick Ross, pp. 10-11; Chris H. Galbraith, p. 11 (left); Agamaphotography, p. 11 (right); Peter Barritt/ SuperStock, pp. 12-13; Dennis Donohue, p. 12 (top); Ronnie Howard, p. 12 (middle); Tom Reichner, p. 12 (bottom); Cristi Bastian, pp. 14-15; Samuel Strickler, pp. 16-17; Richard Cummins/ SuperStock, p. 17 (left); Spirit of America, p. 17 (right); David R. Frazier/ DanitaDelimont.com Danita Delimont Photography/ Newscom, p. 18; Val Thoermer, p. 19; Mark Weber/ Age Fotostock/ SuperStock, pp. 20-21; Megan Carley, p. 21 (top); Steve Bly/ Alamy, p. 21 (bottom); Joe Gough, p. 22; ElenaGaak, p. 22 (small); Robyn Mackenzie, p. 23; Joe Kline/ AP Images, pp. 24-25; Age Fotostock/ SuperStock, p. 25 (small); Steve Smith/ Newscom, pp. 26-27; Vblinov, p. 27 (left); Tish1, p. 27 (right); Pakmor, p. 28 (top); Julia Remezova, p. 28 (bottom); Kaspri, p. 29 (left); Steve Byland, p. 29 (right).